CONTENTS

LAKE CLASSICS

*Great British and Irish
Short Stories I*

Robert Louis
STEVENSON

Stories retold by Prescott Hill
Illustrated by James McConnell

LAKE EDUCATION
Belmont, California

LAKE CLASSICS

Great American Short Stories I

Washington Irving, Nathaniel Hawthorne, Mark Twain, Bret Harte, Edgar Allan Poe, Kate Chopin, Willa Cather, Sarah Orne Jewett, Sherwood Anderson, Charles W. Chesnutt

Great American Short Stories II

Herman Melville, Stephen Crane, Ambrose Bierce, Jack London, Edith Wharton, Charlotte Perkins Gilman, Frank R. Stockton, Hamlin Garland, O. Henry, Richard Harding Davis

Great British and Irish Short Stories I

Arthur Conan Doyle, Saki (H. H. Munro), Rudyard Kipling, Katherine Mansfield, Thomas Hardy, E. M. Forster, Robert Louis Stevenson, H. G. Wells, John Galsworthy, James Joyce

Great Short Stories from Around the World I

Guy de Maupassant, Anton Chekhov, Leo Tolstoy, Selma Lagerlöf, Alphonse Daudet, Mori Ogwai, Leopoldo Alas, Rabindranath Tagore, Fyodor Dostoevsky, Honoré de Balzac

Cover and Text Designer: Diann Abbott

Library of Congress Catalog Number: 94-075357
ISBN 1-56103-032-5
Printed in the United States of America
1 9 8 7 6 5 4 3 2

❦ Lake Classic Short Stories ❧

"The universe is made of stories, not atoms."
—Muriel Rukeyser

"The story's about you."
—Horace

Everyone loves a good story. It is hard to think of a friendlier introduction to classic literature. For one thing, short stories are *short*—quick to get into and easy to finish. Of all the literary forms, the short story is the least intimidating and the most approachable.

Great literature is an important part of our human heritage. In the belief that this heritage belongs to everyone, *Lake Classic Short Stories* are adapted for today's readers. Lengthy sentences and paragraphs are shortened. Archaic words are replaced. Modern punctuation and spellings are used. Many of the longer stories are abridged. In all the stories, painstaking care has been taken to preserve the author's unique voice.

Lake Classic Short Stories have something for everyone. The hundreds of stories in the collection cover a broad terrain of themes, story types, and styles. Literary merit was a deciding factor in story selection. But no story was included unless it was as enjoyable as it was instructive. And special priority was given to stories that shine light on the human condition.

Each book in the *Lake Classic Short Stories* is devoted to the work of a single author. Little-known stories of merit are included with famous old favorites. Taken as a whole, the collected authors and stories make up a rich and diverse sampler of the story-teller's art.

Lake Classic Short Stories guarantee a great reading experience. Readers who look for common interests, concerns, and experiences are sure to find them. Readers who bring their own gifts of perception and appreciation to the stories will be doubly rewarded.

🌾 Robert Louis Stevenson 🌿
(1850–1894)

About the Author

Robert Louis Stevenson was sick with tuberculosis from an early age. In spite of this—or perhaps *because* of this—he lived a life of imagination and adventure.

Stevenson traveled more than most people. One reason was his search for a place where his health might improve. Rainy Scotland, which he dearly loved, was the one place he could not stay.

On one of his trips, Stevenson met a widow, Mrs. Fanny Osbourne. He followed her from France to the United States and married her there. Then he, his wife, and his stepson sailed a schooner to Hawaii. Next they sailed to Australia, where Stevenson became very sick and almost died.

Eventually the Stevensons settled in Samoa. The climate there suited both his health and his romantic spirit. Among the Samoans, he became known as *Tusitala*, the teller of tales. He spent his last four years there—writing in the quiet of his mountain home, *Vailima*.

Stevenson could never work more than a few hours a day for a few days in a row. Most of his writing had to be done as he rested in bed. But he turned out some of the most memorable stories in English literature. Among these are his novels *Treasure Island* (1883), *Kidnapped* (1886), and *The Strange Case of Dr. Jekyll and Mr. Hyde* (1886). In 1885, *A Child's Garden of Verses* was published. It remains one of the world's most popular collections of poetry for children.

Stevenson died as he said he would like to die—hard at work on a book. He lies buried in Samoa.

Stevenson once wrote, "There is no duty we so much underrate as the duty of being happy." If reading good stories is something that makes you happy, then it is your duty to read on!

A Lodging for the Night

Would you take pity on a hungry stranger? On a snowy night in Paris, an old soldier shares his food and his fire. The last thing he expects is an argument about honor.

"Leave them to their game," Villon whispered. "My poem is more important."

A Lodging
for the Night

One winter night long ago, the snow fell silently and steadily on the streets of Paris. It was the coldest night of the year. The city's poor people looked up at the sky and wondered where so much snow could be coming from.

François Villon, a poet, had an answer. "Somebody in heaven must be plucking a goose," he said. "It isn't snow that we see falling, but goose feathers!"

The four rough-looking men sitting with François began to laugh. Nicolas, the oldest, had a fat face that was mostly covered by a white beard. He slapped François on the back and said, "I was just like you when I was young. I would make jokes about everything!"

François smiled and held out his empty glass to the old man. Nicolas picked up a wine bottle from the table and filled the glass.

It was late at night, and the men had been in the little house for a long time. Who wanted to go outside on a night like this? It seemed much nicer to stay indoors by the fire, talking and laughing.

Outside the house there was no talking or laughing. The house was set against a wall at the back side of a large cemetery. At midnight, two men from the police patrol passed by the cemetery. They did not know about the men in the house. The shutters were closed, so no light could be seen coming from the house. The smoke from the fire was lost in the falling snow. The patrol passed by the cemetery without stopping.

Villon sat at the table with a piece of paper in front of him. Every now and then, he would laugh and write down a few words. He was making up a poem that he called "The Ballad of Roast Fish."

Villon was a short, thin man with long black hair. He looked older than his 24 years. His face was sharp and ugly. There was an evil look to it, something wolf-like. And in his eyes there was something of the pig—something greedy.

Next to him sat Nicolas and Guy Tabary, a man with a mashed nose. Tabary watched with interest as Villon wrote the poem. Tabary himself had no skill at writing poems. He was a thief, and had no time for such things. Still, he thought Villon was very clever to be able to write poems so easily.

The two other men in the room, Montigny and Pensete, were playing cards at a nearby table.

Montigny was different from the others. When he spoke, his voice was softer. His clothes were clean and pressed. Something about him hinted that he had come from a good family.

Pensete's looks gave people another idea. He was bald on the top of his head, with curly red hair on the sides. His eyes were tiny slits. He looked like a fox who was about to steal a farmer's chicken. He smiled as he looked at the money he had won so far. "Do you want to play double or nothing?" he asked Montigny.

Montigny nodded, but there was no smile on his face.

Villon had no interest in the card game at the other table. "Listen," he said to Nicolas and Tabary. He picked up the paper he had been writing on and began to read:

Some may prefer to dine in state,
On bread and cheese on silver
*   plate—*

Then he stopped reading for a moment. "Someone help me with this poem," he said with a laugh.

Tabary and Nicolas both laughed too.

Quickly Villon wrote some more. Then he read what he had written:

Or parsley on a golden dish—

Outside the wind was beginning to blow harder. It whipped the snow about in a wild dance. It made a howling sound in the chimney of the little house.

"Can you hear that howling?" Villon said to the other men in the room. "What an awful noise! It sounds like the devil is hanging thieves and murderers."

He looked at Nicolas and winked. "I think it will be cold tonight on Saint Denis Road, don't you?"

Nicolas laughed. Saint Denis Road ran in front of the gallows where thieves and murderers were hanged.

Tabary laughed too. In fact he laughed so hard his face got red.

Villon reached out his hand and pinched Tabary's nose, which made the other man howl.

"Enough of that!" he said to Tabary. "I need help finding a rhyme for *fish*."

At the other table, Pensete won yet another game of cards.

"Let's play double or nothing again," said Montigny.

"With all my heart," Pensete said, nodding and smiling.

"Is there any more wine in the bottle?" Nicolas said.

"No," Villon told him, "so let's open another one. But I don't think you will ever be able to fill up that fat body of yours."

He turned to Tabary and pinched his nose again. "Come on," he said, "think of something to rhyme with *fish*. You know how to think, don't you? You had better learn before your time comes to meet the devil."

Villon stopped teasing Tabary and looked at Pensete and Montigny. Then he whispered to Tabary and Nicolas, "Speaking of the devil, take a look at Montigny. He looks as angry as Satan himself. He must have lost again."

Montigny's face was bright red, and his mouth was shut tight. He was breathing fast, as though he was afraid of running out air.

Tabary whispered, "He looks as if he could kill Pensete."

"Leave them to their game," Villon whispered. "My poem is more important. Let me see—how does it go again?" He began to tap his hand on the table as he read from the paper in front of him.

Then he, Tabary, and Nicolas heard a

grunt. They looked over at Montigny and Pensete.

Pensete had just won again—but he would not enjoy his winnings. Montigny had gotten to his feet and pulled a knife from his pocket. Then, with one quick movement, he stabbed Pensete in the chest. Pensete didn't even have time to cry out. The knife blade went right to his heart, killing him at once.

All four living men sprang to their feet. First they looked at the dead man, and then they looked at each other in shock.

"My God," said Tabary, and he began to pray aloud.

Villon broke out into crazy laughter. He looked at the dead man again, and then sat down in his chair. His head dropped to the table and he began to shake all over.

Montigny was the first to recover from the shock. "Let's see what he has on him," he said, going over to the dead man. Quickly he picked the man's pockets and put the money on the table. The money was then divided into four equal piles. "Everybody gets a share," he said, taking one of the piles.

Nicolas was next to act. He reached for his own share and put it in his pocket.

"We are all in this together," Villon said. "It's a hanging job for all of us." Then he pocketed his share of the money.

Tabary was last to help himself. He scooped up the rest of the money and sat down in a corner of the room.

Montigny looked at the body of the man he had just killed. Then he looked at the three other men. "You fellows had better get moving," he said.

"I think we had," said Villon, with a gulp. "But something is bothering me." He pointed at the dead man. "Look at him! What right has a man to have red hair when he is dead?" Then he started crying so hard he had to sit down. He put his hands over his eyes and bent over double.

Montigny, Tabary, and Nicolas started to laugh aloud.

"Crybaby," said Nicolas.

"I always said he was just a little baby," said Montigny. "Now, sit up, can't you?"

While Villon was bent over, Nicolas went over to him and picked his pocket.

Montigny and Tabary both looked at Nicolas and made faces. It was clear that they wanted a share of the money he had taken from Villon.

Finally Villon shook himself and jumped to his feet. He went over to the fire and began to put it out.

Montigny opened the door a crack and looked out to the street. The coast was clear. There was no police patrol in sight. He turned to the other men. "We had better slip out of here one at a time."

Villon stepped forward. "I will go first," he said. The others could see that he was in a hurry to get away from the dead body. That was fine with them. They wanted him to go before he found out that his money had been stolen.

The snow no longer fell, and the wind had died down. The moon was full and shining bright. Villon wished the snow had not stopped falling. It would have covered his footprints. He was afraid the police might be able to follow his tracks.

As he walked along, he thought about two things. First, he thought about the gallows at Saint Denis Road. Second, he thought about the face of the dead man. In his mind, he could clearly picture the white skin and red hair. Both thoughts sent shivers through him.

As he walked, he kept looking back over his shoulder. But he was the only moving thing on the white streets. Suddenly he saw a pair of lights swinging in the distance. As he got nearer, he could see the shapes of the men who carried them. It was a police patrol!

He did not want to meet up with them. In a panic, he looked around for a hiding place. Then, on his left, he saw a great hotel. It was an old building that was empty and in ruins. In three steps he was inside and out of sight of the patrol.

It was dark inside. As he moved slowly through the darkness, he stepped on something. It gave him a scare, and he jumped back a few steps. Then he waited for his eyes to get used to the dark. He gave a laugh when he saw that it was only the body of a woman who had frozen to death. It was nothing to be afraid of.

Villon quickly searched the dead woman's body. Her pockets were empty, but there were two small coins tucked in her shoe. For a moment, he held the coins in his hand and looked down at her. What a pity that she had not had time to spend the coins! It was not much money—but it was something. When he died, he did not want to have *anything* left over.

He started to put the two coins in his purse. Then he gave a cry. For an instant, his heart stopped beating and a feeling of cold came over him. He felt as though he had been hit on the head.

His purse was missing!

As Villon thought about it, he began to sweat. His share of the dead man's money was gone. With it, he had felt like a king. Now he felt empty. He knew he was in danger of being hanged for the murder of Pensete. He had not stuck the knife in—but he had been there when it happened. And now it was all for nothing!

He cursed and stamped his feet on the

floor of the old hotel. Then he stepped into the street and threw the two coins into the snow.

He headed back to the house where the murder had taken place. No longer was he worried about the police patrols. All along the way he looked for his purse, but without luck. Nothing was to be seen. He had not dropped it in the street.

When he got to the house, he cursed again. Earlier he had tried to put out the fire in the fireplace. But he had not succeeded. In fact the fire had spread, and now the whole house was on fire.

He went back to the hotel and hunted for the coins. But he could find only one of them. The other was buried too deep in the snow. Besides being angry, he was getting very cold. He feared he would end up like the poor old woman who had frozen to death.

What was to be done? Maybe he could stay at St. Benoit's Church. Sometimes people were allowed to stay there to get out of the cold. But now it was probably much too late to get in. Still, it was worth a try. When he got to the church, he tapped on the door. There was no answer. He knocked louder. Still, there was no answer. Then he began to bang again and again on the door. At last he heard steps coming near.

"Who is there?" cried out a voice from inside. Then a small window in the door opened, and a man looked out at Villon.

"It's only me," said Villon.

"Oh, it's only you, is it?" the other man said in an angry voice. "Why do you come banging at our door at this time of night?"

"I'm so cold that my hands are turning blue," Villon said. "My feet are numb from the snow and my nose aches from the sharp air. I may be dead before morning. Let me in just this once and I will never ask again!"

"You should have come earlier," the man said. "Young men like you need a lesson now and then." He shut the window and locked it.

Villon banged on the door with his fists and kicked at it with his feet. "Wormy old fox!" he cried. "If I could get my hands on you, I'd give *you* a lesson or two!"

He turned away from the church. Well, he thought, that was life. It would do him no good to stand around crying in the cold. What was to be done? It looked like he had a night in the frosty streets ahead of him.

Just then he thought of the woman who had frozen to death. The picture in his mind gave him a sudden scare. What had happened to her might happen to him before morning. Surely he was too young to die!

He thought of visiting some old friends who lived nearby. But he didn't think they would be too happy to see him. He had made fun of them in his poems. He had also cheated them out of some money, come to think of it. But there was one who might forgive him. It was a slim chance, but it was worth trying.

On the way there, two little accidents happened that made him think.

First, he saw the fresh tracks of a police patrol in the snow. The patrol must have crossed his tracks and kept going. That was good news. It meant they weren't following him.

Second, he passed a place where wolves had once attacked and killed a woman. The thought scared him. This was the kind of weather that brought wolves into the city. A man all alone didn't have a chance against a pack of wolves.

Years ago his mother had showed him the place. His mother! If he knew where she lived now, he could ask to spend the night there. Maybe he'd ask somebody tomorrow if she were still alive.

Just then he came to the house he was looking for. It was dark, like all the houses around it. He tapped on the door a few times. From inside a voice asked, "Who is there?"

"It is me, François Villon," he said.

He waited for a minute or so, and then heard a window opening above him. He looked up just as someone dumped a pail of water out of it.

He tried to step out of the way, but water splashed all over him.

The window slammed shut.

Villon cursed again as his wet clothes began to freeze. This is it, he thought, as he headed off down the street. He would die for sure unless he found a warm place! Well, nobody was going to invite him into a house. He would have to break into one!

He looked across the street and saw a house that would do. It looked dark at first. Then Villon saw a little twinkle of light coming from a window.

"The devil!" he thought. "Why are they still awake? Don't they know it's way past bedtime for decent people?"

Then he laughed out loud. "Well," he thought, "if they're still up, maybe they'll give me some supper!"

He walked up to the house and banged on the door. There was no point in hiding. Since he wasn't going to break in now, why be sneaky?

Soon he heard footsteps coming to the door. And then the door was opened wide. A tall man stood in the doorway. His head was large, and the lines on his face showed that he was old. His white beard was neatly trimmed. He was a fine-looking man.

"You knock late, sir," the old man said to Villon in a polite voice.

Villon held his hat in his hands and said how sorry he was.

"You look cold," said the old man. "I bet you are hungry, too. Please come into my home."

Villon stepped inside, and the old man closed the door behind him.

"Please follow me," the old man said. He turned and started up the stairway to the second floor.

The upstairs room was warmed by a fire in a large fireplace. Villon stepped near the fire and rubbed his hands together. Then he put his back to the fire and looked around the room. There was not much furniture in the room. A couple of chairs were next to a small table near the fireplace. In one corner stood a cabinet that held a number of gold cups. There was a bookcase against one wall. A large painting of a mountain scene hung over the fireplace.

"Will you seat yourself?" said the old man. "Please forgive me for leaving you, but I am alone in the house tonight. In a few minutes I'll be back with something for you to eat." Then he turned and left the room.

No sooner was the old man gone than Villon got up from his chair. He started looking around the room carefully. Pulling back the curtain, he looked at the window. It was made of stained glass. Villon figured it must have cost plenty. Then he went to the bookcase and looked at all the books. Some of them were very old. They might bring a good price.

He went over to the cabinet and picked up a gold cup. He bounced it in his hand as he counted the others. "Seven," he said. "If there were ten of them, I might risk it."

Just then he heard the old man's footsteps. He hurried back to his chair.

The old man brought in a plate of bread and meat and a bottle of wine. He set the meal on the table. Then he went to the cabinet and got two gold cups.

He filled the cups with wine and made a toast. "I drink to your better luck," he said, touching Villon's cup with his.

"To our better friendship," said Villon. He drank from the cup, then set it down. Without another word, he began to eat the bread and meat.

The old man looked his guest over carefully. Then he said, "You have blood on your shoulder, my friend."

No! Villon thought. Montigny must have touched him with his bloody hand!

"It was none of my doing," Villon said to the old man.

"I did not think so," the old man said. "Was there a fight?"

"Well, something of that sort," Villon said.

"Perhaps a fellow murdered?" the old man asked.

"Oh, no, not *murdered*," Villon said quickly. "It was all fair play—killed by accident. I had no part in it, believe me."

"Well, probably another bad fellow out of the way," the old man said.

Villon felt relieved. "Yes," he said, "he was as bad a man as you could find. Still, it was an awful sight to see. I will bet that you have seen many dead men in your time."

"Yes," said the old man. "I used to be a soldier and have been in many wars."

Villon set down his knife and fork. "Did any of them have red hair?" he asked. "The man I saw murdered had red hair. I knew him. Seeing him lying there dead really bothered me."

"Have you any money?" asked the old man.

"I have one coin," Villon said with a

laugh. "I took it from a woman who had frozen to death. Winter is a very hard time for poor women, wolves, and men like me."

"Something is strange," said the old man. "You seem to have learning. You do not seem like a criminal—yet you take money from a dead woman. Is that not a kind of theft?"

"It is the kind of theft that often takes place in wars, sir," Villon said.

"But wars are fought on the field of honor," said the old man. "In war a man risks his life for God, his king, and his country."

"Does not a thief also risk his life?" asked Villon.

"For gain, but not for honor," said the old man.

"Gain?" Villon said. "The poor fellow wants supper, and takes it. But so does a soldier in wartime. When he needs anything, he takes it from wherever he can find it. He doesn't care who he takes it from. He takes food, and he takes money. And often he takes it from people who have little of either."

"Sometimes that must be done in time of war," the old man agreed. "It is just one of those things that poor people have to live with. It is true that some soliders are no better than thieves."

"You see?" said Villon. "It's hard to tell soldiers from thieves. I take a lamb chop from a kitchen and nobody notices. There is always plenty left for the other people to eat. But a soldier comes up to a farm and takes the whole sheep. The farmer's family may go hungry. But the soldier says he is taking it for God, king, and country! I am only a thief, and hanging is too good for me. But just ask the farmer which one he would rather see. Ask him which one makes him angriest."

"Look at the two of us," the old man said. "I am old and honored. If I were to lose my house, hundreds would take me in. The poorest person would give me shelter. But you walk about the street without a home. You are not welcome anywhere. I fear no man. You sneak about like a dog. When I die, people will weep. You will probably die by hanging— and people will cheer. Don't you see the difference between us?"

"Yes," said Villon. "But what if I had been born rich, and you had been born poor? I would live in a great house like this. You would be digging for small coins in the snow. *I* would be the soldier, and *you* would be the thief."

"A thief?" cried the old man. "*I a thief!* If you knew what you were saying you would take the words back."

"Wait a minute," Villon said. "You have not paid attention to what I was saying."

"Enough!" said the old man. "Learn to hold your tongue when you speak with your betters." He got up and stared into the fireplace, his heart filled with anger.

Villon filled his cup again and sat back in his chair. He felt good. He was warm now, and no longer felt hungry. He had almost made it through the night.

The old man turned from the fire. "Tell me one thing," he said. "Are you really a thief?"

"Since I am your guest, I will tell you the truth," Villon said. "Yes, sir, I am a thief."

"You are very young," the old man said.

Villon held up his ten fingers. "If I had not used these hands to take what I wanted, I would not be as old as I am."

"You can still change your ways," the old man said.

"I think of it every day," Villon said. "But until things begin to change for the better, I will not change, either."

"The change must begin in your heart," the old man said.

"Do you think I steal for the fun of it?" Villon said. "I hate stealing, just as much as I hate work. I shake every time I see the gallows. But even a poor man like me must eat and drink. If someone made me rich, I would never steal again. But as long as I am a poor poet, I must stay the same."

The old man returned to the fireplace and stared at the blaze again. Then he turned to Villon once more. "Listen to me," he said. "I know that hunger is hard to bear. But honor, love, and faith are more important. All you think about is filling your belly with food and wine. It would be better to fill your heart with higher things."

Villon was growing tired of the old man's talk. "You think I have no sense of honor!" he cried. "It's hard to see rich people with fancy gloves when you can't keep your own hands warm. An empty belly is harder to bear than you think. If you had had as many hungry nights as I, you would change your tune. I'm a thief, it is true—but I'm not a devil from hell. My honor is as good as yours. I just don't talk about it so much."

Villon pointed at the cabinet. "You told me you were alone in the house. Did I try to steal your cups? You are old, and I have a knife. But I didn't try to kill you. I came in here poor. I'm ready to go out as poor as I came in. And you say I have no sense of honor!"

"I will tell you what you are," the old man said. He shook his fist in the air. "You are a thief and a bad fellow! I wish I had never let you into my house. You make me sick!"

"Very well," said Villon. He stood up

and finished his cup of wine. "I believe you are a man of honor. I wish I could also say that you were a smart man—but I can't."

The old man followed Villon down the stairs to the front door.

"Good-bye, old man," Villon said as he stepped outside. "Many thanks for the supper."

The door closed behind him. The sun was just starting to rise over the white roofs. It was still very cold in the city. Villon stood in the street and stretched his arms wide.

"A very dull old man," he thought. "I wonder how much his gold cups are worth."

❧

Markheim

Do you think "the hand of heaven" ever reaches down and touches human lives? In this story a cold-blooded criminal has unexpected company. Have the police broken down the door? Or is this the kind of visitor who doesn't use doors at all?

THE DEALER FOUND MARKHEIM'S WORDS HARD TO
BELIEVE. STILL, HE WELCOMED THE CHANCE TO MAKE
MONEY.

Markheim

"Yes," said the dealer, "I sometimes get very good buys. Some customers are ignorant, and my greater knowledge helps me. Some are dishonest—and that helps me, too." He held the candle up so that the light fell on Markheim's face. "I profit by being honest."

Markheim had just come into the shop from the daylight. His eyes had not grown used to the darkness inside. He blinked at the dealer's words and looked away.

The dealer chuckled. "You come to me on Christmas Day," he said, "when you know I am closed for business and alone in my house. Well, you will have to pay for that. I should be balancing my books right now. You will have to pay for my loss of time. And when a customer can't look me in the eye, he has to pay for that, too."

The dealer laughed again. "So, show me what object you want to sell today. I am sure you can tell me where you got it. You always have a good story."

The dealer was a short man with a pale face. Now he stood on tip-toe and leaned forward to see what Markheim had brought.

Markheim shook his head. "This time I have not come to sell, but to buy. I am in no need of money. I have done well in the stock market just lately. Now I want to buy a Christmas present for a lady."

Markheim spoke as though he had practiced the speech many times. "I am sorry to bother you when you are closed. I meant to get the gift yesterday, but I was too busy. It is very important that I give it to the lady at dinner tonight. As you know, a rich marriage is greatly to be wished for."

The dealer said nothing at first. The only sound in the shop was the ticking of a dozen clocks. The dealer found Markheim's words hard to believe. Still, he welcomed the chance to make money. "Well, sir," he said to Markheim, "you are an old customer. If you say you have a chance for a good marriage, I am glad to be of help."

The dealer bent down behind the counter and came up with a fancy mirror. "Here is something nice for a lady," he said. "It was sold to me by a young man much like yourself."

Markheim's hand shook as he took the mirror from the dealer. "A mirror?" he said. "A *mirror*? For Christmas? Surely not!"

"And why not?" cried the dealer. "Why not a mirror?"

Markheim had a strange look in his eye. "You ask me why not?" he said. "Look in it—look at yourself! Do you like what you see? Are you happy with the way you look? No! Nor am I—nor is anyone!"

The little man had jumped back when Markheim had raised his voice. Now he smiled at Markheim. "What does your future wife look like—if she's afraid of mirrors?"

Markheim didn't think the dealer was funny. "I ask for a Christmas present," he said, "and you show me this! People think too much when they study their own faces. They think of the past—all their mistakes, all the bad things they have done. Did you mean it? Had you really thought about it? Tell me. Are you a kind man?"

The dealer looked closely at his visitor. If this was meant as a joke, Markheim did not appear to be laughing.

"What are you getting at?" the dealer asked.

"Do you mean you are *not* kind?" Markheim said. "Do you mean you are not a loving man? You are only interested in money—is that it?"

An angry look came to the dealer's face. "I will tell you what it is," he said. "I think you have been drinking!" Then his look changed. He spoke in a softer voice. "It must be because you are in love."

"Ah!" Markheim said, "have *you* ever been in love?"

"Have I ever been in love?" said the dealer. "Oh, no. I have never had the time, nor do I have time today. Do you want the mirror or not?"

"Where is the hurry?" said Markheim. "It is very pleasant to stand here talking. Life is so short. I would not hurry away from any pleasure—even such a small one as this. We should hold on to what little we can get. Let us talk to each other and trust each other. We might even get to be friends."

"I have just one thing to say to you," said the dealer, coldly. "Either buy something or get out of my shop."

"True, true," Markheim said. "Enough fooling. Let's get down to business. Show me something else."

The dealer bent down again to put the mirror back. Markheim moved a little closer. Then he reached into his coat pocket and leaned over the counter. There was an ugly look on his face. It was filled with terror, horror, anger.

"This might suit you," the dealer said, starting to stand up.

But just then Markheim pulled his hand from his pocket. It held a knife. His arm moved forward in one fast motion.

The dealer gave a short cry and fell backwards, hitting his head on a shelf. He was dead before he hit the floor.

The only sound in the shop was the ticking of the clocks. Markheim noticed that the clocks all had different voices. Together they made a kind of music. Just then he heard a boy running by on the sidewalk outside. The sound of his footsteps took Markheim by surprise. He looked around the shop as though seeing it for the first time.

The candle stood on the counter, its flame dancing. Shadows moved slowly on the walls of the room. At the back of the room a door stood ajar. A long slit of light—like a pointing finger—showed through the crack.

Markheim wondered if there might be somebody in the next room. But no, that could not be. He knew the dealer had a servant—a young girl. But he had seen her leave the house a few minutes earlier. No doubt she was off to visit her family for Christmas. She would not be back for quite some time.

His eyes returned to the body on the floor. It lay there in a heap. The dealer seemed much smaller now that he was dead. Markheim thought he would feel fear at the sight of the body. But it was nothing. It seemed no more than a bundle of old clothes. It would never move again. It would lie there in the shop until somebody found it.

Who would find it? The servant? Then she would tell the police, and they would try to find the killer!

Just then, the clocks began to strike

the hour of three in the afternoon. Some of the chimes rang out in high tones, some in low.

The sounds from all those clocks startled Markheim. He picked up the candle and moved about the room. Now he saw that there were mirrors on all the walls. Some were held in fancy frames, some were much simpler. But Markheim saw his face in all of them. And in each mirror, his eyes stared back at him as though they could see through him.

Markheim filled his pockets as he moved about. There were many things in the shop that he could sell for a good price. Here a gold watch, there a silver spoon.

As he did his work, he began to think of his mistakes. He should have picked a better time than this. He should have prepared an alibi. He should not have used a knife. He should have only tied

up the little dealer, not killed him. Or—
he should have also killed any servant
that might be in the house.

His worries began to grow stronger.
They scurried like rats in the attic of his
mind. He thought of what it would be like
if the police caught him. First he would
go to jail. Then he would be hanged. And
then he would be put in a black box and
buried!

He began to worry about the people in
the street outside the shop. Had anyone
heard anything? Had they heard the
dealer cry out? Had they heard him
strike his head and fall to the floor?

He thought about all the people in the
houses nearby. Right at this moment
they might be sitting quietly, listening.
Just an hour ago they might have been
thinking of past Christmas Days. But no
longer. Now they would be wondering
about the sounds from the shop. They

would be thinking about the dead man and the evil man who killed him. They would be thinking of the rope that would hang the killer!

He tried to move through the shop without making any noise. But when he picked up two gold cups, they hit together with a ringing sound. He thought it must sound like an alarm to anybody nearby. Even the ticking of the many clocks upset him now. He wished he could stop them all. Then his fears took a different turn. Maybe it was *too* quiet in the shop. That might make people wonder.

He began to move about more boldly. He thought a little noise would seem more natural. If anybody was listening, they would think it was the dealer going about his business. But then the first fears came back. He began to move about slowly, making almost no sound at all.

Suddenly yet another fear took hold of him. It was not fear of somebody in a nearby house. And it was not fear of somebody walking by outside. Those fears seemed distant to him now.

What if somebody else was in the house? What if the girl had come back early from shopping? Was that possible? No, that was a foolish worry. She would have had to come through the shop. He was alone. And yet, he thought he heard footsteps coming from somewhere in the house. Were they in the next room? No. Were they coming from upstairs? He listened closely. No, not from there either. No, he decided, there were no footsteps. What he thought he heard was all in his own mind.

From time to time, he would glance at the open door. The pointing finger of light did not move. And yet, Markheim seemed to see shadows dancing there.

Suddenly, from the street outside, came a banging on the door. The jolly voice of a man rang out. He cried out the dealer's name. "Open up and let me in," he said. Then he banged on the door again.

Markheim felt his blood turning to ice water. He glanced at the dead body on the floor. Was the dealer really dead? Could he possibly hear the noise? No! He lay quite still. He was far gone from the sounds and cares of the world.

After a while, the man outside went away. But his short visit had made Markheim think. He was taking too much time. One visitor had come already. Who could say that another might not come at any moment?

In a panic, Markheim thought of running off without filling his pockets. But that idea passed quickly. The deed was done. It would be foolish not to get something for it. Now he must find where the dealer kept his money.

He looked over at the open door again. Did he see a shadow behind it? No. The shadow was only in his mind.

He went over to the dealer's body and looked down at it. No longer did the heap on the floor look to him like a human being. It seemed like nothing more than a suit of clothes, stuffed with cotton. And yet Markheim felt a shiver of fear. He wondered what would happen if he touched it. Carefully, he lifted the body by the shoulders and turned it on its back. He was surprised at how light it was. The face had no expression on it. It was as pale as a white wax candle, with a dab of blood at the temple.

The blood bothered Markheim. It made him remember something he had seen as a boy. It was a day that a fair had come to his town. In his mind now, he could still hear music and the beating of a drum. One booth at the fair had paintings that showed famous criminals and their victims. The bloody pictures had scared him terribly then. They had almost made him sick to his stomach. Those scenes all came rushing back to him now.

Should he run away and hide? No! He made up his mind to resist the feeling. He must deal with his fears, as strong as they might be. Markheim stared into the face of the man he had just killed. A short time back that face had been filled with life. But he had put out all the life in it. He had stopped the dealer's beating heart as one might stop the ticking of a clock.

Markheim felt a bit of pity for the dealer. That man had not lived his life to its natural end. Now he was dead. But the man's blood did not sicken him as the bloody pictures had. Markheim felt no regret for killing him—none at all. It was something he had to do. His mind turned back to the money. Quickly he found a set of keys in the dead man's pockets. He took them and headed for the open door.

Hard rain began to fall outside the house. The sound of the rain mixed with the sound of the ticking clocks. As Markheim got near the door, he thought he heard another sound. Was that a footstep on the stairs? He stopped for a moment. Then he moved forward quickly and pulled open the door. He could see across the room to the stairs. There was nobody there. He stepped into the room and looked around. Works of art were hanging on the walls. There were carvings made from some kind of dark wood. There were old paintings in gold-painted frames.

As he took in those sights, the rain

came down even harder. Markheim seemed to hear all kinds of sounds in the drumming of the rain. Was that the sound of soldiers marching in the street? Were those the sound of footsteps coming from upstairs? He could not lose the feeling that he was surrounded by other people. He heard them upstairs. He heard them in the street. He even heard a terrible sound coming from the shop— it was the dead man getting to his feet!

No! He knew that could not be. *All the sounds were in his mind.*

He went over to the stairs and began to climb. Suddenly he wished that he were deaf. At least then he could feel some peace. Then just as suddenly he changed his mind. He was glad that he could hear. His hearing would save him from getting caught. Was he on the edge of madness? When he reached the top of the stairs, he saw a long hallway. There were three doors in the hallway, all of them ajar. To Markheim they all looked like traps.

He wished that he were home in his own house, where only God could see him. That idea made him remember something. He had heard that many murderers feared they would be punished by a heavenly hand. But that was not his fear. Markheim was afraid that he would leave some clue to his crime. Even more, he feared that nature would play a trick. Maybe lightning would start a fire! When the firemen came to put it out, they would surely find him.

But as he thought about it, he changed his mind. Maybe a trick of nature *would* be the hand of heaven!

No! He changed his mind again. He did not fear God's punishment. God would know why he did what he had to do. It was only men that he had to fear.

Markheim stepped into the first door in the hallway. The room was not in very good order. There was no rug on the floor. Chairs and tables were all around the room, but none of the furniture matched. Framed paintings stood with their faces to the wall. Packing cases were scattered here and there. In one corner was a large cabinet with a padlock on the door. Perhaps that was where the dealer kept his money. Markheim thought it was worth a try. He sat down in one of the chairs and started looking through the keys.

Now and then he glanced at the door he had closed behind him. The strange thing was—he was not really worried. In truth, he felt at peace now. The rain falling in the street sounded natural and pleasant. Now he could hear children singing a hymn. He thought there must be a church nearby. He smiled as he listened to the music. It made him think of the days when he went to church as a boy. He remembered how the parson's voice had sounded as he read the Ten Commandments.

Suddenly he heard a sound that sent a flash of fear through him. He heard footsteps coming slowly up the stairs. Was it the dead man walking? The footsteps came closer and closer, until they were just outside the door. Markheim stared at the door and saw the knob turn. Fear held Markheim in its grip. He had no idea what to expect. It might be an officer of the law, or just someone who had dropped by for a visit. He heard a click, and the door swung open. Markheim had never before seen the man who stepped into the room. The visitor smiled at Markheim and said, "Hello, did you want to see me?"

Markheim stood up and stared at the man. Maybe he *had* seen him before. There was something about him that seemed familiar. Could it be that he looked a little bit like Markheim himself? A lump of living terror filled Markheim's heart. Then another thought filled his mind. Maybe this thing was not of the earth—and not of God. Yet the creature seemed like an ordinary man you might see any day on the street. Again he smiled at Markheim and said, "You are looking for the money, I believe."

Markheim did not answer.

"Mr. Markheim," the other said, "I must warn you that the servant is on her way back from the store. If she finds you here—I think you know what will happen."

"You know me?" cried Markheim.

The visitor smiled. "You have been a favorite of mine for a long time," he said.

"I have often wanted to help you."

"What are you?" cried Markheim. "Are you the devil?"

"What I may be does not matter," said the other. "It has nothing to do with the help I want to give you."

"Yes, it does!" cried Markheim. "How could I be helped by you? No, never—not by *you*. You do not know me yet. Thank God, you do not know me!"

"Oh, I *do* know you," said the visitor in a firm voice. "I know you to the soul."

"Know me?"cried Markheim. "How can you know the real me? All you can know about me is what shows on the outside. I have done many bad things, but not because I wanted to do them. The world has not treated me fairly—so I *had* to do those things. Can you not understand that I hate to do evil? Can you not see that I am an unwilling sinner?"

The visitor shook his head. "I do not care *what* makes you do what you do," he said calmly. "I am only interested in the fact that you *do* such things. But let us not waste time talking. The servant girl will be here soon. So—shall I help you? Shall I tell you where to find the money?"

"For what price?" said Markheim.

"You may think of my help as a Christmas present," said the visitor.

Markheim could not keep from smiling. "No," he said, "I will take nothing from you. It may be hard to believe, but I will never make a deal with the devil."

"Well," said the visitor, "you can always take it all back on your deathbed."

"You say that because you do not think it would do me any good," Markheim said.

"I look at it differently than you," the visitor said. "All I care about is that you do the evil deeds while you are alive. What do I care if it makes you feel better to change your mind when death is near? That is your business. You can ask God to forgive you, if you want."

"Do you think that is what I want to do?" said Markheim. "Do you think I want to sin and sin and sin—and then sneak into heaven? Is this what you think I want? Do you think that because I have committed murder there is no good in me at all?"

"Murder is nothing special to me," the visitor said. "To me, all sins are the same. I am not so much interested in bad acts, but in bad men. I am not interested in you because you have killed the dealer. I am interested in you, Markheim, because of the kind of man you are."

"You are wrong!" Markheim cried. "I have committed my last crime. In the past I have done bad things only because I needed money. But today I have gained both riches and wisdom. From now on I am a changed man."

"I think you plan to use this money to invest in the stock market," the visitor said. "But that is how you have lost all your money in the past."

"Yes," Markheim said, "but this time it will be different."

"No," said the visitor, "you will lose it all again."

Markheim began to sweat. "Well, what if I do?" he said. "I can earn more—even if I have to commit another crime. That would still not mean that I love evil. A part of me might, but that is not all of me. Although I have committed the crime of murder, I am not without pity. I pity the poor—and who understands them better than I do? I love goodness, too. I love the sound of honest laughter. I love all good and true things on earth."

The visitor raised a finger. "For 36 years you have been in this world," he said to Markheim. "In all that time I have watched you fall. Just 15 years ago the thought of theft would have made you sick. Three years ago you would not even think of murdering someone. But now you are different. Is there anything you would *not* think of doing? And five years from now, what will you be like? Down, down, down, you go—and nothing but death will stop you."

"It is true," said Markheim, "that I have done some evil things in my life. But everyone does."

"I will ask you a simple question," the visitor said. "From your answer, I will be able to tell what lies ahead for you. *Have you become a better man in any way, or have you become worse in all ways?*"

"Better in any way?" said Markheim. "No," he said sadly, "I have gone down in every way."

"Then," said the visitor, "you should be content with what you are. You will never change."

Markheim said nothing.

At last the visitor broke the silence. "That being so," he said, "shall I show you the money?"

"And will God forgive me?" asked Markheim.

"Have you not already tried that?" said the visitor. "Two or three years ago I saw you in a church. You were singing hymns and praying louder than anybody. But it did not make any difference, did it?"

"It is true," said Markheim. "You have opened my eyes. At last I see myself for what I am."

Just then there was a knocking at the shop door downstairs.

"Listen!" said the visitor. "The dealer's servant has returned to the store. You must go down and let her in. Tell her that her master is sick and needs to see her. Once she steps inside the door, you know what to do. Get rid of her the same way you got rid of him. Then you will have nothing to fear. You can spend all night looking for his money. Go now! Do what you must do!"

Markheim looked the visitor in the eye. "If all my acts have been bad, there is still one door to freedom open to me. I can stop acting at all. If my love of good cannot help me, maybe my hatred of evil can. I know this will anger you, but I will take strength from my hatred of evil."

As Markheim left the room and headed downstairs, the visitor smiled. The look on his face changed in a wonderful way. No longer was it the look of a devil, but that of an angel. His whole face grew brighter and brighter. Then he faded away and was gone.

Markheim thought about his past as he walked across the shop to the door. Indeed his life had been ugly and filled with bad deeds. But he saw peace ahead.

The knocking came again.

Markheim opened the door and saw the servant standing there. He greeted her with something like a smile.

"You had better go for the police," he said. "I have killed your master."

Thinking About
the Stories

A Lodging for the Night

1. Are there friends or enemies in this story? Who are they? What forces do you think keep the friends together and the enemies apart?

2. Did the story plot change direction at any point? Explain the turning point of the story.

3. How important is the background of the story? Is weather a factor in the story? Is there a war going on or some other unusual circumstance? What influence does the background have on the characters' lives?

Markheim

1. Many stories are meant to teach a lesson of some kind. Is the author trying to make a point in this story? What is it?

2. An author builds the plot around the conflict in a story. In this story, what forces or characters are struggling against each other? How is the conflict finally resolved?

3. What period of time is covered in this story—an hour, a week, several years? What role, if any, does time play in the story?

Thinking About
the Book

1. Choose your favorite illustration in this book. Use this picture as a springboard to write a new story. Give the characters different names. Begin your story with something they are saying or thinking.

2. Compare the stories in this book. Which was the most interesting? Why? In what ways were they alike? In what ways different?

3. Good writers usually write about what they know best. If you wrote a story, what kind of characters would you create? What would be the setting?